River of Life

by **Debbie S. Miller**
Illustrated by **Jon Van Zyle**

Clarion Books • New York

ACKNOWLEDGMENTS

Thanks to Dr. Mark Oswood, Sue Quinlan, and the many biologists who helped me better understand the web of life that surrounds our rivers. I'm also grateful to the late Dorothy Briley, an editor who believed in this story and the promise of the next draft. Without her vision, this book would not be.

Clarion Books
a Houghton Mifflin Company imprint
215 Park Avenue South, New York, NY 10003
Text copyright © 2000 by Debbie S. Miller
Illustrations copyright © 2000 by Jon Van Zyle

The illustrations were executed in oil paint.
The text was set in 15-point M Hiroshige Medium.

For information about permission to reproduce selections from this book,
write to Permissions, Houghton Mifflin Company,
215 Park Avenue South, New York, NY 10003.

Printed in Singapore.

Library of Congress Cataloging-in-Publication Data

Miller, Debbie S.
River of life / by Debbie S. Miller ; illustrated by Jon Van Zyle.
p.   cm.
Summary: Describes a river in Alaska and the life that it supports, emphasizing how the living things
around it are connected and dependent upon it for their survival.
ISBN 0-395-96790-2
1. Stream ecology Juvenile literature.   [1. Stream ecology. 2. Ecology. 3. Zoology—Alaska.]
I. Van Zyle, Jon, ill. II. Title.
QH541.5.S7M54   2000
577.6'4—dc21   99-38350
CIP

TWP   10 9 8 7 6 5 4 3 2 1

Icy snowflakes blow and swirl. They wrap the mountains in sparkling layers of white. A river whispers beneath the snow, tucked in by a sheet of winter ice.

4

5

*S*pring comes. The sun grows warm and bright. One by one, the snowflakes begin to melt. *Drip, trickle, gurgle, swish.* Silent ice turns to water, sending the river with a hundred voices to the sea.

6

*O*ld spruce trees bow to the river. The leaves of cottonwood trees flutter above the rushing water. Their roots drink the melted snowflakes. Trees and willow bushes hold the nests of many birds. *Sweet-sweet-sweet-sweet.* A bright yellow warbler sings in harmony with the rippling river.

*S*almon fry swim in quiet pools that are shaded by the trees. They eat plankton and tiny insects. *Splash, slip.* A harlequin duck dives underwater and probes for caddisfly larvae and other insects in the streambed.

A kingfisher sends its loud rattling call above the river. He wears a bluish-gray feathered crest. He catches wiggly salmon with a beak that looks too long for his head. Beneath the surface, a rainbow trout chases salmon fry. The trout catches a glimpse of something shiny. Will it take a bite?

*T*he curious child peeks at a moose sipping from the river.
Shadows dart beneath the water's surface. Big fish chase little fish.
A trout swims right beneath the moose. *Splash!* He slaps water into
the moose's face. The child covers his mouth and giggles.

Summer days grow warmer. Hungry eagles, bears, otters, and people search for salmon that swim up the river to spawn. Eagles catch them with their sharp talons. Brown bears and otters use their teeth and claws.

Watchful ravens cackle and caw. Gulls cry and squabble. They follow the river, searching for scraps of salmon, picking what's left off the bones. A red fox scares off the birds and eats his share.

The soil along the river smells rich and fishy. It holds the bones of salmon, the scat of many animals, and the mushy leaves that have fallen from the cottonwood and birch trees. It is home to worms and ants, beetles and bugs, mosses and mushrooms. A robin plucks out a fat worm. A vole gnaws on an old moose antler.

22

Wildflowers bloom in the rich soil by the river, bringing visitors to their bright faces. *Buzz. Flutter. Bzzzzz.* Bumblebees and butterflies drink the sweet, sticky nectar. Dragonflies zigzag above the flowers, catching mosquitoes.

23

The tiny seeds of the flowers and grasses dance with the autumn wind. A junco hops along the ground, feeding on the seeds. *Plop. Plop.* Watch out, junco! A red squirrel is about to toss another cone from the crown of a spruce tree. The squirrel will eat the seeds of the cones through the long winter.

25

26

Golden cottonwood leaves tumble from their branches. The trees give their leaves, needles, and twigs to the river and the earth. They will slowly decay, feeding a world of tiny insects. Those insects will become a meal for a newborn salmon, a hungry bird, or a probing shrew.

Snowflakes blow and swirl once again, wrapping the mountains in sparkling layers of white. A sheet of winter ice tucks in the whispering river.

Many birds fly south, raven stays.

Grizzly bear hibernates, moose survive the cold.

The earth and all its living things will be patient until the sun melts the snow and the river rushes to the sea once again.

Glossary

Rivers are the lifeblood of the land. There are more than 3,000 rivers in Alaska, fed largely by melting snow and glaciers. This book describes the biodiversity, or web of life, of a typical river along the southern coast of Alaska. Perhaps you can find a river or stream near your home or school and discover all the plants and animals that are interconnected within its vibrant habitat.

Brown bear: Coastal brown bears often feed on a rich diet of salmon. These bears are larger than inland brown bears, known as grizzly bears. When salmon are plentiful, coastal male bears eat an average of eight fish per day, although one hungry bear was once observed catching 90 fish in one day! An estimated 32,000 brown bears live in Alaska.

Caddisfly: During its larval stage, this insect lives inside a tubelike case made of leaves, sand, twigs, or tiny pebbles. It often feeds on fallen leaves in rivers. Aquatic insects and their larvae are an important source of food for many fish and birds.

Dragonfly: The four-spotted skimmer dragonfly is Alaska's official state insect. Dragonflies dart through the air chasing mosquitoes and other prey. Their huge, bulging eyes can help them to spot a mosquito forty yards away. Dragonflies have lived on the earth for millions of years. Some of their ancestors had a wingspan the size of a raven's.

Harlequin duck: These multicolored ducks are found on many of Alaska's rivers and along rocky coastal areas. They appear to enjoy floating down the rapids of swift rivers. Harlequins dive and probe for insects in the streambed.

Junco: This slate-colored bird hops on the ground, picking up seeds near the edge of the forest or in brushy, open areas. Male juncos have a distinct breeding call that sounds like a telephone ringing.

Kingfisher: The belted kingfisher is a long-beaked bird that is easily recognized by its rattling call. These birds dive for small fish along rivers. They lay their eggs underground, often at the end of a tunnel in a river bank. Parent birds teach their chicks how to catch fish.

Moose: Moose are found along many of Alaska's rivers and streams, where they browse, or feed, on the leaves and twigs of willows, birches, and aspens. The large trees that grow along rivers also provide shelter and snow cover for moose and other animals.

Mosquito: Mosquitoes are an important source of food for dragonflies and many birds. People dislike these insects because female mosquitoes feed on the blood of humans and other warm-blooded animals. But this blood-rich diet is essential to the mosquitoes' ability to grow and to lay their eggs.

Mushroom: Mushrooms are fungi that play an important role in the web of life. Some mushrooms help trees grow. *Amanita muscaria,* the orange mushroom pictured in this book, has a symbiotic, or mutually dependent, relationship with birch trees. The mushroom's fine rootlike hyphae (pronounced *Hi-fee*) transport nutrients to the tree roots, while the tree's sugars nourish the hyphae. This mushroom is poisonous to humans.

Plankton: These microscopic plants and animals drift through the water, providing food for fish and other animals. Animal plankton are known as *zooplankton.* Plant plankton, such as algae, are known as *phytoplankton.*

Rainbow trout: This trout is one of the most abundant freshwater species of fish. Some rainbows, known as steelhead trout, spend part of their lives at sea. Juvenile rainbows feed on insects and crustaceans. The diet of a grown trout consists mostly of small fish.

Raven: A respected bird, described in many Native American stories and legends, ravens are seen year-round in Alaska. These hardy scavengers are intelligent, social, vocal, and acrobatic. They cartwheel, roll, and tumble through the sky. Even on a day when it's 50 degrees below zero in Alaska, you can see ravens and hear their caws and croaks.

Red fox: Red foxes can be found in most of Alaska. They feed on voles, hares, birds, eggs, and berries. Unlike wolves and coyotes, which run down their prey, foxes stalk their prey, then spring in the air and pounce on it. Foxes also scavenge, feeding on animal carcasses, such as salmon.

Red squirrel: During the summer, red squirrels spend much of their time cutting and storing piles of green spruce cones. The piles, known as middens, can contain many thousands of cones. The seeds of cones are a major source of the squirrel's winter food.

Robin: Some red-breasted robins migrate to Alaska in the spring to nest and feed. They are often spotted on the ground snatching insects, grubs, and worms.

Salmon: There are five commonly known species of salmon that live in Alaska's waters. Each species has two familiar names: king/chinook, silver/coho, pink/humpback, red/sockeye, and chum/dog. Salmon are anadromous (pronounced *a-NAD-ruh-mus*) fish. *Anadromous* is a Greek word that means "running upward." Salmon hatch in freshwater, spend part of their lives in the ocean, then "run up" the river or stream to their birthplace to spawn.

Salmon fry: Fry are small fish that have recently hatched and emerged from the gravel beds of streams or rivers. They feed first on microscopic zooplankton, and later on aquatic insects, such as mayfly nymphs.

Tree: Trees play an important role in keeping a river and its aquatic life healthy. Their roots prevent soil erosion. Spruce trees provide shade and shelter for juvenile fish. Cottonwoods and other trees shed leaves that provide food for aquatic insects. Trees also provide an important habitat for many mammals and nesting birds along the river corridor.

Vole: This mouselike mammal sometimes gnaws on bones and antlers, good sources of calcium.

Yellow warbler: These small, beautiful songbirds are found throughout most of North America. In Alaska, they often construct nests in willow shrubs or in trees growing along a river. On average, they weigh around nine grams—about as much as nine paper clips—yet they migrate thousands of miles between Alaska and their winter home in Central or South America.

DATE			